We Need to Talk

A Practical Guide
for Those Facing Terminal Illness

Larry E. Quicksall

FamilyGrowth™
Publishing
Effingham, Illinois

We Need to Talk:
A Practical Guide for Those Facing Terminal Illness
Copyright © 2002 by Larry E. Quicksall

Requests for information and book orders
should be addressed to:

FamilyGrowth Publishing
1310 N. Keller Drive, Suite 9, Effingham IL 62401
217-347-5937
books@familygrowth.org

ISBN: 0-9719475-0-3 (paperback)

Printed in the United States of America

For Aaron & Jessica

Table of Contents

Acknowledgments i

Introduction ii

Emotional Expression of Loss 1

    Grief 1
    Shock 7
    Denial 8
    Anger 13
    Bargaining 15
    Guilt 17
    Depression 21
    Acceptance 23

Caring for the Patient 26

    Curative Care vs. Comfort Care 26
    Pain Control 27
    Nausea 32
    Constipation 34
    Dehydration 36
    Artificial Feeding 38
    Oxygen 41
    Medical Equipment 42

Caring for the Caregiver 44

    For Caregivers 44
    For Family & Friends of the Caregiver 48

Items of Importance 50

    Advanced Directives 50
    Final Arrangements 58
    Children and Funerals 65
    Preserving Your Memories 68
    Alternatives and Herbal Treatments 70

The Three Phases of Terminal Illness 72

    Phase 1 – Introductory Phase 72
    Phase 2 – Work Phase 74
    Phase 3 – End Phase 77
    Early Signs of Approaching Death 78
    Later Signs of Approaching Death 79
    Active Dying 81

Closing Thoughts 83

About the Author 84

Acknowledgments

First and foremost, I want to thank God for the unexpected opportunity to work in the field of terminal illness. It has been a blessing that has impacted my life in many ways.

I also want to thank my family for their patience and encouragement while writing this book. Everyone needs cheerleaders, and they have been great.

I cannot thank my colleagues in the hospice field enough for the guidance, teaching, encouragement, and support they have provided me over the years. We have shared pain and joy, loss and hope, ignorance and wisdom, and we have grown through it all. My heart continues to be with you as you reach out to those who need it most. Thank you so much.

Finally, I want to thank all of my hospice patients and their families. You allowed me into your homes and your lives at the most challenging time in your lives. We laughed and cried and grew together. You taught me so much about living that I will always be grateful. I look forward to our chance to meet again on the other side of death where *"He will wipe every tear from their eyes. There will be no more death or mourning or crying or pain, for the old order of things has passed away,"* Revelation 21:4.

i

Introduction

If you are reading this book, you are probably facing a situation that you would rather not be facing. Most likely, either you or a loved one has been told by your doctor that there is nothing more he can do for you. He may have suggested palliative or hospice care. He may or may not have given you a time frame. You may have been expecting something like this or it may have been the greatest shock you have ever had. In any case, you are likely experiencing a variety of feelings that can range from shock to anger to fear. You may not have any idea of what to expect or what you should do from this point forward. But, rest assured, you are not alone.

Terminal illness is a phrase used when a person's disease is unable to be cured and it is expected to eventually cause the person's death. It is a time that involves a lot of change for both the patient and their family. In this book, I will provide you with basic information on facing terminal illness. I realize that the subject is not a comfortable one to discuss, and certain things you may not be ready to think about. That is all right. You can read this book at your own pace as you become ready to address the various aspects of terminal illness.

In this book, I will address emotional expressions of loss, caring for the patient, caring for the caregiver, various items of importance, the phases of terminal illness, and the physical signs of approaching death. It is written and indexed so you can jump around the book to find what you need to address what you are experiencing.

I hope you find this book beneficial as you face this very challenging time in your life. Please know that my thoughts and prayers are with you and your family.

Larry E. Quicksall

Emotional Expression of Loss

Grief

Grief is often something that we experience but rarely truly think about because it is usually uncomfortable to do so. In this section, I am going to ask you to think about the uncomfortable as we try to gain a better understanding of this, at times, overwhelming emotion.

Simply put, grief is an emotional response to the pain and fear of a lost relationship. In a broad sense, we can experience grief about any type of relationship including people, animals, objects, and fantasies, though I will be specifically addressing the grief involved with losing relationships with people.

Anticipatory vs. Post-Mortem Grief

There are a variety of observations we can make regarding the grief experience. A person can experience grief before and after a death, depending upon the circumstances. For example, in a sudden death, such as a car accident, grief is experienced post-mortem, after the death. However, when someone is diagnosed with terminal cancer, the grief experience nearly always begins prior to the death, and we call this anticipatory grief.

Anticipatory grief can be experienced in a variety of ways depending upon the type of relationship that is involved and

1

how the person's illness is impacting that relationship. If a relationship is distant or if the activities of the relationship are not seriously affected, the person may experience very little anticipatory grief. However, if a relationship is intense or if the activities of the relationship are dramatically affected, then the person will likely experience significant anticipatory grief. Let me offer a couple of personal examples to help illustrate this point.

Several years ago two of my elderly family members became terminally ill: a great uncle and a grandfather. While I got along very well with each of them, I was much closer to my grandfather than with my great uncle. I remember seeing my great uncle for the last time at his home. We had light conversation, told a few humorous stories, and shared some tears when it was time for me to go. While there was sadness, the grief did not have a noticeable impact on my day-to-day life. On the other hand, my grandfather was a different story. I had a close relationship with him over the years, and in his final months that relationship began to change due to what the doctor described as small strokes that he was experiencing every few weeks. These strokes affected his memory and reasoning, and it eventually resulted in hallucinations. Every time I saw him a large part of our relationship changed. I experienced a great deal of both anticipatory and post-mortem grief with Grandpa.

Pace of Grief

We do not progress through grief at the same pace as others. Some grieve quickly while others appear to be walking through deep snow. It is often our coping skills and previous experience with the grieving process that will most influence our pace of grief. As with any skill, the more

2

positive experiences you have with it, the better able you are to handle it. The opposite is also true when we have few experiences with grief or a history of bad ones.

Let me offer another personal example. My grandmothers died in 1988 and 1993, and in both those circumstances my experience with anticipatory grief was not that good due to numerous complications. As a result, I had grief related difficulties that lasted longer than they should have. Later, in 1994, I made a career change and began working for our local hospice organization. In that position, I provided anticipatory grief counseling and assisted families in preparing for the patient's final weeks and eventual death. At hospice, I had received training and ongoing peer support, and learned by teaching others. With that understanding and support I was able to cope much better with grief than before.

In my opportunities to work with grieving families, I have found that everyone appears to progress at a different pace in dealing with grief. These differences can easily cause problems in family relationships. I believe that people generally like to go through most things at the same pace. For example, when a group takes a walk together they can easily begin to spread-out over the path with faster ones taking the lead and slower ones lingering behind. When this happens you begin hearing people say things like "Hey, slow down up there," and "Come on slow-poke! You're holding everyone up." Well, if you listen to grieving families you can hear similar statements designed to try to keep everyone grieving at the same pace. For example, when someone is progressing faster through grief we may hear comments accusing the person of being in denial or not caring about the loved one. And for the slow ones, we can hear people exclaim that they won't let go of the past, need to get out more, or are in need of help to get over this. Granted, each of these accusations could be true in the given situation, but my experience has lead me to believe that the majority of the time the problem is with the accuser not feeling comfortable with the other person's pace of grief.

The fact of the matter is people grieve at different speeds. Some will progress quickly and others slowly, and that is OK. Family members and friends need to be supportive and allow the person's grief to progress at its own pace. If there is a question or concern about an individual's pace, then consult with a competent grief counselor who can assess the situation and offer wise counsel as to how to progress.

Grief Reactions

People generally react to grief in the ways they react to other losses. If you want to know whether a grief reaction is normal for a person, just ask yourself whether the person has reacted to other losses in a similar manner. For example, if a person typically reacts to loss with anger, then you might expect the person to express anger when grieving the current situation. Other common grief reactions besides anger include depression, withdrawal, preoccupation with work or school, exerting control, sadness, crying, denial, guilt, and running away. Sometimes a person's reaction may be quite different and may be due to a complication or an aversion to end of life situations.

How Long Does Grief Last

How long does grief last? It depends. Some people will progress through their grieving process in a matter of days while others may take several months. For the death of a very close family member, such as a spouse or child, the grief process may last one to two years as they experience holidays and special events without sharing them with their loved one. The second year should show signs of significant healing for the survivor. When it doesn't or if the grief reaction is severe, the person will likely benefit from individual or group grief counseling.

Tips for Coping with Grief

The best suggestion I can give for coping with grief, whether anticipatory or post-mortem, is to talk about it. Find someone who will listen to you without necessarily giving you advice on how to "fix it." You need to get the issues outside of yourself to better deal with them. It seems that the more we keep traumatic situations inside, the more emotional distress we experience. There is an old saying that I come to believe more and more every day, and that is "A joy shared is a joy doubled, and a grief shared is a grief halved." When we share with a trusted person, whether it is good or bad, we cope with the situation better than if we try to deal with it in isolation.

When working with a family, I am often asked what they are to share about the situation. There are four steps that I like people to share when experiencing grief. **The first step is to describe what they have been experiencing.** In other words, tell the story as they have lived it. In an initial conversation, it may be the whole story, while in later ones, it may just be an update of the last few days. In my general counseling practice, I find that many people experience a relief in simply telling the story of what they have been going through. **The second step is to describe the feelings and emotions that you experienced during the situation(s) that you just described.** How did it feel to go through the situation? What emotions did you experience? Did it remind you of other situations? Try to remember the feelings from the experience, because it builds into the total picture that you described in step one. **The third step is to describe your present feelings and emotions now that some time has passed since the experience.** Have your feelings changed with the passing of time? Do you see the situation differently, and if so, how? In your opinion, are your emotions better or worse with the passage of time? **Finally, in the fourth step, you describe how you would like to handle the situation if or when you have to experience it again?** This step points us into the future with a better sense of perspective from the past.

You can work through these steps in a variety of ways. You can meet with a family member, close neighbor, or friend and let them help guide you through these steps. Others may not have a person in their natural support system that can work with them on these steps, so they may need to seek the assistance of a social worker, bereavement counselor, pastor, or priest. Some people may find themselves in situations where finding someone with whom to have such a conversation is next to impossible. In those cases, I encourage them to follow these steps in a journaling exercise. Take 20 minutes each day to sit quietly, reflect, and write down your thoughts following the four steps outlined above. When you are done writing for the day, read them out loud to God. He is always there to listen. Also, read over some of your writings from previous days, and when you feel like you have made progress in coping in a particular area of grief, place a star in the upper corner of the page as a way of noting that you are moving in a positive direction. Journaling can also be an excellent means of enhancing your conversations with others as suggested above.

In addition to journaling, as a way to cope with post-mortem grief, I have had people write letters to the deceased. Sometimes life does not permit us an opportunity to tell our loved one everything we needed to prior to their death. In those situations, I have suggested that they write a letter or series of letters to the deceased, sharing with them the good and the bad. Sometimes the relationship with the deceased was very problematic, and writing a letter is too painful. If you find yourself in that situation, please seek the support of a bereavement counselor or therapist who can help you move through the process of complicated grief.

Shock

Few things can shake you to the core as hearing the doctor pronounce that you or a loved one is going to die. The words that the doctor uses can vary from the vague to the specific, but when the message finally sinks in, it can affect you in such a way that you do not know how to react. Generally, shock is what most people initially experience when they hear "the news," and they can react in a variety of ways. Some common responses during a shock phase include silence, withdrawal, "thousand mile stare," panic, hysterics, and unusual calm. In a way, shock is like eating a hot pepper: some people will immediately spit it out while others try to ignore the fire in their mouth and just swallow it down. Those who experience the panic and hysterics appear to be initially "spitting out" the news, while those who withdrawal appear to be detaching from it and trying to "swallow it down."

Why do we experience shock? It seems that when a message is too much to handle, we can experience some level of shock. Shock is not necessarily a bad thing. It appears to

7

be a mechanism that lets us adjust to the change at a slower pace. Shock is typically not a long phase for people and can last from a few hours to a few days. The length of the shock period can vary depending on a number of factors including how close you are to the person who is terminally ill, whether the prognosis was expected, and how well the person copes with change or bad news.

When someone is experiencing shock, and many times several people in the family are experiencing it together, I recommend three things: time, support, and comfort. Shock takes some time to run its course, so do not try to rush yourself or another person through it. Those experiencing shock need supportive people who are present and can be there for them. Supportive people do not need silver tongues that offer words of wisdom; in fact most people find such comments counterproductive during the shock and grieving process. Support can be tending to the phone, making a meal, or watching the children or grandchildren. Comfort refers to the little things that we can do, so the people do not find themselves in isolation. Comfort can be sitting with a person, sharing a meal, listening to them, and validating their feelings without trying to fix the situation.

Remember, not everyone will experience shock as described above. If a person is anticipating bad news, what the doctor tells them may actually be a relief, even if the news is of a terminal nature.

Denial

Denial is when we do not want to believe something to the point that we ignore reality and sometimes embrace fantasy.

Emotional Expressions of Loss

We can experience denial to varying degrees and at different points in the anticipatory grief process, and at times denial can be severe enough to cause major problems for the patient, family or healthcare providers.

Denial, like shock, is a phase that is not necessarily bad and appears to allow us to more slowly absorb the news that we did not want to hear. As I think back over various families that I have worked with over the years, I tend to see several specific types of denial. One type I call "initial denial," and it tends to occur just after the shock phase starts to wear off. Initial denial can be seen in statements like the following:

"The doctor can't be right. I feel fine. You can't believe lab results like these."

"He's too young to die. I am not going to lose my son. We'll get a second or third opinion. I am not going to just believe any doctor."

"She's still taking chemotherapy, so there has to be a chance. We have to keep our spirits up. We have to trust God. He hasn't let us down before. He won't let us down now."

Initial denial appears to happen when the prognosis is so far from what we consider possible, or even acceptable, that we run from it and take up a defensive posture against it. Imagine if you will a soldier caught off guard by the enemy. His initial response is to seek cover and shoot back at the enemy. This same kind of reaction appears to be what happens during initial denial. A doctor tells a person that she is going to die, and the statement initially catches her off guard and may result in an experience of shock. Once the

9

shock starts to wear off, she then takes cover and looks to identify and attack the enemy. The enemy is generally anyone who supports or accepts the notion that she is going to die. The first attacks are typically directed at the doctor and other healthcare professionals. The second strike is then often directed at family or friends who are not experiencing denial as she is.

What happens next depends upon whether the person experiencing denial looks to reality or fantasy. When the person looks towards reality, they gradually start moving towards accepting their diagnosis and prognosis. I am not saying the person likes what they see, but the denial is not as strong as reality, and they believe more and more the truth of what is actually happening to them. If the person starts to move towards fantasy, then she and her family can experience a growing multitude of problems, due to the fact that the decisions they make regarding the illness and the future are not based in reality but fantasy and falsehood. In some cases, the person can become delusional where they are unable to see, believe, or accept the obvious.

I remember one sad situation where an adult child was being cared for by his parents. For the mother, the possibility that her child would die prior to her own death was impossible to conceive. The patient was aware and accepting of his terminal condition, and so were other family members. However, because of the severe denial in the mother, all family members were dancing a very uncomfortable dance to appease her. No one was permitted to say anything implying that he would die. Hospice was conditionally admitted to the home with the stipulation that we did not mention end-of-life issues in her presence. Everyone was expected to be cheery and hopeful for her child's recovery.

During the week prior to his death the patient slipped in and out of consciousness, and still the mother insisted that he would pull through. As you can probably imagine, she fell apart when her son finally died and for days after the funeral she tried desperately to hold onto her denial by repeating that he was not supposed to die. I find it amazing just how strong denial can be when we are stuck clinging desperately to a fantasy that cannot come true.

You may be wondering how the hope for a miracle fits into this process. Let me be up front and say that I do believe in miracles. I have a strong Christian faith and do believe that God will at times cure the incurable to bring greater glory to himself. I have seen such miracles take place, and I have had the unusual pleasure of discharging several people from hospice, because they were no longer terminally ill. However, I also know that hope and desire does not always bring a cure. More times than not, the person dies, but that does not mean that a miracle did not occur. I remember a conversation I had with an elderly father regarding his dying son. He shared with me his constant prayer to God for a miracle. As he wiped away tears he said, "I kept praying and looking for a miracle, but I was looking in the wrong place. The miracle was who my son became because of the cancer." His son had led a very rough life, and the cancer opened his son's eyes to the kind of person he had been over the years. His final months witnessed a dramatic change in his personality that his father could only describe as a miracle. While he was going to miss his son greatly, he was so proud of him for the person he had become at the very end of his life.

Another type of denial occurs as the terminally ill person progresses in their disease and requires additional assistance and support. In this progression denial, the person does not deny that the condition is terminal or that the person will eventually die. What appears to happen is that the person with denial accepts where the patient is in their disease progress, but denies that they will get worse. For example, a wife may deny that her ill husband has progressed to the point of needing a hospital bed and demands that he continues to sleep where he has been. Another example could be a husband who, despite the fact that he is unable to walk across the room without losing his breath, refuses to discuss having oxygen in the home for comfort measures. Those in the medical field often see this type of denial triggered by a suggestion or need for anticipated equipment such as canes, walkers, oxygen, commodes, and hospital beds. It is as if keeping the equipment out of the home keeps the disease at a distance. Unfortunately, when this denial persists, the patients can find themselves in physically dangerous situations. When carried to an extreme, some family members have been charged with elder neglect because of this type of denial.

As I said at the beginning of this section, initial denial is not necessarily bad. It can slow the change to allow a person to eventually accept what is happening. However, what happens when the denial is hurting the patient? When I worked as a hospice social worker, I sometimes felt as if I was in a spin-off of the movie Ghostbusters, where the slogan was, "Who ya gonna call... Denial Busters."

At times you cannot wait for denial to run its natural course, and in those cases it may be necessary to break through denial in a particular person or even an entire family.

The common term for this process is an "intervention." The goal of an intervention is to confront the person or persons with a carefully metered dose of reality that breaks through the fantasy of denial without causing emotional damage to the person. It is not something I recommend just anyone do. You can have a variety of unpredictable responses as a result of the process, so I only recommend mental health therapists with experience in this area conduct interventions. Your local hospice organization, mental health agency, or a private therapist may be able to assess for and provide necessary intervention services. It has been my experience that most intervention requests are not necessarily needed, and that with some guidance and time the person can move out of denial.

Anger

I think anger is one of the most difficult emotions for family members to deal with. Many of us have an image of our loved ones going through their last weeks and days peaceful without any extreme emotions. This is a nice fantasy, but is not very realistic. Generally, people cope with situations at the end of their life just as they have during the majority of their life. Most people, when they have something taken away from them, get upset. They may become quite angry and will often express it in a pattern consistent with what they have practiced over their lifetime. Some people explode, while others may get quiet, moody, or resentful.

The terminally ill person is having their life taken away from them, and unless they are ready to give up their life, they are likely to become upset. Generally, they will express their anger as they typically would in other situations. However, in this case there is often an additional frustration: who to blame.

13

Where does the patient, and family members for that matter, focus their anger? Maybe in your situation there is an obvious person to blame, or maybe there is no clear guilty party, and in that case, it can feel like you are holding a hot potato with nowhere to set it down.

Logical targets for anger can include doctors, spouses, God, cigarette companies, employers, product manufacturers, and themselves. However, the typical recipients of anger are those closest to the patient and can include spouse, children, caregivers, and healthcare staff. Receiving such anger can be very overwhelming. I have seen patients abandoned by family members, because they could not take the anger and verbal abuse of the patient anymore.

Working through and talking out the anger is important to be able to move towards a greater sense of peace. Having a trusting individual to talk to about the anger is the first step. The talking partner may be a family member, pastor/priest/rabbi, neighbor, friend, social worker, nurse, or even home health aid. The listener needs to do just that: listen. The initial need to have someone listen is greater than to get direction or advice. It's kind of like cleaning out the old food from a neglected refrigerator. First, you have to remove all the old food and wipe up any old spills before you begin putting back the good food. Let the angry person talk the anger out before you start helping him see things in a better light. If you need some assistance in helping a family member, contact your local hospice or counseling agency, and they should be able to give you some specific suggestions and coaching.

Bargaining

Bargaining is a phase of anticipatory grief that people sometimes find themselves experiencing. It is not just for the terminally ill patient, because family members can often find themselves bargaining to a greater degree than the patient. I tend to think of it as two people haggling over the price of a precious object that one person desperately wants to buy. The important question that must be determined is whether the object is for sale. If it is not for sale, the bidder can work himself into a frenzy trying to up the price in hopes of getting it. We can see the same thing in terminal illness when a person desperately wants to live.

When a person enters the bargaining phase, he typically begins by running through a list of everyone he believes who can possibly grant him a cure or at least an extension on his life. This list commonly includes their doctor, any physician specialists, nurses, pastors and priests, and God. If the answer appears to be "no" from each of these, the person must make a decision: do I accept their authority and expertise or do I seek out other options? If a person decides to seek out other options, he may find himself going in a variety of directions, both orthodox and unorthodox.

I am not going to promote or condemn any particular option that a person chooses to pursue, but I will caution everyone to these two points: (1) desperate people will often choose desperate means, and (2) there are always going to be people who will take advantage of desperate people. I would encourage anyone considering various options to pursue logic and wise counsel before making dramatic decisions. I have personally known people who have sadly lost thousands of dollars on cancer-cures cooked up in kitchen sinks of foreign

15

countries that did nothing but offer false hope. I have also known people who bought additional time or were given a clean bill of heath through experimental treatments. I remember one elderly pastor's wife who had survived several bouts of cancer over the years, and I had the pleasure of discharging her from hospice after her cancer spontaneously disappeared without any curative medical treatment, just a lot of prayer.

When our bargaining does not appear to be working, and our illness continues to progress, we have another choice to make: move towards acceptance or revert to denial. If we move towards acceptance, we accept the reality that in spite of all of our efforts we will succumb to our illness. We can now begin to change our relationship with death from something to be avoided at all costs, to a less than comfortable relationship that we must learn to deal with. However, if we choose to revert to denial, we are abandoning the logic of reality for the blind hope of fantasy.

People who revert to denial often find it difficult to accept other aspects of reality. I remember one gentleman whom I met with to explain the hospice program. He was very polite, but after I had made my presentation, he stated that he could not accept any hospice or home care services, because to do so would be abandoning his trust in God to cure him completely. Please hear me, I am a strongly spiritual man and firmly believe that miracles do occur, but I also know that each of us will eventually die. I believe that this gentleman reverted to denial because of he refused to consider a logical approach to his situation and he refused to accept help for problems he was currently experiencing. Sadly, this gentleman died approximately three weeks later leaving his family in shock and bewilderment after having had no practical opportunity to prepare for his death.

Bargaining can be quite exhausting: physically, mentally, emotionally, and spiritually. It is common for people to have "breakdowns" during the bargaining process. It can be easy for some people to be so physically aggressive in pursuing different courses that they reach physical collapse. Others can spend so much mental energy trying to figure out "the answer" that they may be unable to concentrate on or make decisions about the simplest of things. They can have such an emotional desire to find their answer, yet when it continues to elude them they can experience despair and depression. Finally when fervent prayer, convincing faith, and religious ritual seems to fall upon the deaf ears of an omnipotent God, a person's spiritual core can be shaken like a California earthquake.

When breakdowns occur, the person needs patience, calm, rest, quiet support, and wise counsel. It appears to me that when these needs are not met at this critical time, the person can slip into a deep depression and chronic cynicism. They have just completed an exhaustive battle and lost what they were trying to achieve. The war is not over. They need to regroup, develop an entirely different strategy and goal, and prepare to enter the new battle they will face in the very near future.

Guilt

Guilt can be an overwhelming emotion in the grief process. In short, guilt is when we ask the question "what if?" and we do not like the answer because we see the finger of blame pointing back at us. Guilt can be experienced by anyone, including the patient. There seems to be three primary types of guilt: appropriate, inappropriate, and projected. It is important to understand the type of guilt you are experiencing to know what you should do about it.

Appropriate Guilt

The first type of guilt is appropriate guilt, and we experience it because our actions hurt someone else. In my opinion, there is nothing wrong with this type of guilt. Actually, I am greatly concerned if someone does not experience this type of guilt. Appropriate guilt helps us keep our behaviors within the bounds of moral and societal standards. When we experience this type of guilt we should look to see if we could correct the situation, repair the damage, and help the person or people we hurt to be able to forgive us. This does takes courage, but the rewards during this phase of life can be very rewarding.

Inappropriate Guilt

Inappropriate Guilt is guilt that has left the boundaries of logic and is driven by emotion. Often we let ourselves get into a pattern of emotional self-abuse with the goal of punishing ourselves until we feel better about the issue at hand. The problem with this approach is that we never feel better, but instead feel increasingly worse. This type of guilt can become a vicious cycle that spreads into other areas of life.

Projected Guilt

On occasion a person experiencing inappropriate guilt is unable to bear anymore and begins directing it to others. This is called Projected Guilt, and it is characterized by finger pointing, often at those primarily involved with providing patient care. An example might be a daughter who, due to

18

family and work responsibilities, is limited in her ability to help take care of her ill mother. Her sister does not work outside of the home and her children are grown, and so she volunteers to provide the majority of care. The first daughter begins feeling inappropriate guilt because she cannot do as much for her mother as her sister. When she cannot shoulder any more guilt, she becomes increasingly critical of her sister's care giving. She might begin suggesting that the sister is being neglectful or deserves to do more because she does not have kids to take care of anymore. Like the inappropriate guilt, projected guilt is not based in logic, but emotion, and it has the goal of punishing the target until the person feels better, which is not likely to happen.

Savior from Out of Town

When projected guilt is experienced by a person living far away from the ill patient it can be expressed as what I call "Savior from Out-of-Town Syndrome." A savior from out-of-town is typically a family member who is feeling incredible guilt for living far away from the patient, and begins projecting the guilt on the primary caregiver. The savior then comes into town, transfers the guilt into aggressive action designed to "fix" all perceived problems, and then quickly leaves town again. Unfortunately, the typical results include disruption of the care delivery system, hit-and-run emotional or verbal abuse to family members, confusion, hard feelings, and unfinished and unwanted arrangements. After the savior leaves town, she will often blame any remaining or consequential problems on the primary care giver, because when she left town everything was fixed.

An example I remember involved an elderly mother and her two adult children, where the son was the primary care giver and the daughter lived out of state. The daughter had been experiencing inappropriate guilt because she could only visit her mother every few months. As the mother's physical condition declined, the daughter developed projected guilt blaming her brother for the physical decline of their mother. One time while visiting their mother she progressed into a savior and began making major changes to the plan of care without involving her brother in the decision making process. Eventually, this resulted in a situation where the mother was admitted to the hospital without any intention of involving the brother. When the brother eventually learned of what had happened, he found he was not to be informed by hospital staff as to the condition or care of their mother. As this situation unfolded, the savior left town again, abandoning the mother in the hospital, and leaving the brother to pick-up the pieces. While this may appear as an extreme case, it is typical of what can happen in these situations when saviors become consumed with their inability to effectively deal with guilt.

The primary suggestion I would offer to every family is threefold. First, involve all family members in the care giving and care planning process as much as possible. When all family members are actively involved to some degree, there is less likelihood for guilt to grow in isolation. Even out-of-state family members can be actively involved. Try to arrange conference calls for discussing plans or changes to the patient's plan of care. Make sure you provide copies of all written materials by mail to far away family members. Then follow-up the mailings with a telephone call to make sure everyone understands the information. Also, when family members come to town, arrange for them to meet with the health care staff or physician to allow them to answer any questions and to bring them up to speed on the patient's condition. Second, make sure everyone understands and is sensitive to the guilt process, and that they are using logic rather than emotion in dealing with it. Again, inaccurate emotional statements can let inappropriate and projected guilt develop and get out of hand. Third, when you are sure a family is struggling with guilt, promptly get them the professional help they need. The sooner a problem is addressed, the easier it is to correct. Make arrangements for them to meet with the social worker, counselor, pastor or chaplain who will be able to help them with grief issues.

Depression

Depression, which is a common and natural part of the grief process, occurs when we begin to accept that the loss of a loved one is going to happen or has actually happened. It seems to be ushered in when we begin to appreciate all that we are losing because of the death. Depression can occur in both the patient and family members. For example, a patient can experience depression when they begin thinking about what their death is going to mean. They realize that they are not going to be able to experience many things that they hoped to accomplish. They also realize that relationships with loved ones will not be able to continue. At this point, they may have a resurgence of anger, especially toward God, but often the depression pulls them away from the anger. At times, they just do not seem to have the energy to continue with the anger. Family members can experience depression for similar reasons: loss of dreams, loss of growing old together, loss of vacations, and loss of companionship. Likewise, family members can experience anger as they realize all they are losing with the death.

When people experience grief related depression they will commonly withdraw from others, cry, feel sad, and find it difficult to accomplish everyday tasks. Again, this is a natural reaction to the realization that they or someone dear to them is going to die. We should not feel prompted to rescue someone from this kind of depression, but should be supportive to them as they work their way through it. In a way, grief related depression is a unique journey they take through a particularly dark and lonely valley. We can walk along side them as a support, but they must walk through it to reach the other side. What does a person gain by walking through this valley? My observations are that both patients and family members can find themselves gaining a new perspective on life and relationships because of the walk.

Rather than simply calling this phase grief related depression, I will often refer to it as "head-time." During head-time the person may not appear to be accomplishing much on the outside, but they are often working very hard inside. They can be thinking deeply about questions that they have been avoiding their entire life, but cannot avoid any longer. They are often processing important life issues such as:

What does death really mean?

Was life really worth living?

Did I have any meaningful impact on the world?

Will anyone remember me when I am gone?

Why do I have to die?

What happens after death?

Is there a God?

Is there a heaven and hell?

Does God look upon me with favor?

What will happen to my loved ones when I am gone?

Because depression is uncomfortable, the person experiencing it might be tempted to avoid or mask it with whatever is readily available. They may be tempted to use alcohol or prescription drugs to numb the feelings they are experiencing. This should be discouraged for what should be obvious reasons. Providing support to depressed individuals is crucial, but should not be overbearing.

If a person appears to be stuck in a depressed state, a bereavement counselor or social worker may be needed to assess and help move the person towards acceptance. Because each person is unique in his pace of grief, it can be difficult to determine when a person is stuck in depression. Some warning signs can include a progressive worsening of depression, an inability to complete basic life skills, becoming dangerous to self or others, and reporting suicidal thoughts, desires, plans, or attempts. If the person is experiencing these signs, you should contact a social worker, counselor, nurse, physician, or mental health center for assistance.

Acceptance

Acceptance can be described as when a person comes to terms with the anticipated death. It does not mean that the person is looking forward to the death, wanting the death, or desiring the death, but simply that they are accepting that it is going to happen and that it is OK. As I think about acceptance, several people come to my mind. I remember one fellow who wanted to make sure his wife would be taken care of properly after his death. He worked frantically to make the arrangements, and when all was said and done, he found that he could rest and relax until death came. I remember a sweet lady who was living in a retirement home. She had a very close relationship with God, and looked forward to seeing Him face to face. In the meantime, she saw each day of life as an opportunity to pray for others. On her nightstand was a police scanner, and when she heard a police or ambulance call she would begin praying for that person. She performed this valuable prayer warrior task until shortly before her death. I remember another old fellow who was filled with either wisdom or nonsense, depending on who you spoke to. When I first met with him, he appeared to already be firmly standing in acceptance. He understood and accepted his approaching death, and saw it as simply an opportunity to change his priorities. He had reflected over his life, and saw his new primary task as succinctly sharing his knowledge and wisdom with others. I still have a poem he wrote shortly before his death and read it on occasion.

Not every patient has the opportunity to reach acceptance. For some people, death comes too soon or too sudden. However, in these situations, family members often reach acceptance after the loved one's death. They are generally afforded more time to work towards acceptance when their family member is gone. I remember hearing of one lady whose husband had died before they had the opportunity to really enjoy their retirement together. After struggling with anger and depression over the loss of their retirement dreams, she decided to take some of their planned trips alone or with family members in his memory. It was her way of coming to terms with his death. I remember two parents whose infant daughter died resulting in much grief and agony. Following her death, as a sign of acceptance, they planted a special memorial garden to be a physical reminder of their child in heaven.

Do people cry once they reach acceptance? Of course they do. Are they still sad about the death? Of course they are. The main difference is that the person in acceptance is OK with the anticipation of death and has come to terms with it.

Caring for the Patient

One of the greatest tasks that anyone can perform is to take care of and nurture another person. With that said, I am not claiming that the task is an easy one or necessarily a desired one, but nonetheless a truly important task. Care for a loved one who is terminally ill often requires an entirely different approach to care and a different set of skills and abilities. The skills are often the same as we use in other caring situations, but with a different goal and perspective. In this section I will address some of the differences and issues that allow us to adequately care for the terminally ill patient.

Curative Care vs. Comfort Care

When it comes to medical care of the terminally ill, we can divide it into two very different approaches: curative care and comfort care. Curative care is the typical kind of healthcare with which most of us are generally familiar. If you are in a car accident and are taken to the hospital emergency room, you expect the doctors and nurses to do everything possible to save your life. In your rehabilitation, you expect the doctors and therapists to do everything possible to return you to your pre-accident level of functioning. Often it does not matter how invasive, uncomfortable, and costly the procedures, because we want to get back to normal.

Comfort care is entirely different, in that the focus is not to save the patient's life or to return him to the pre-illness level of functioning. Often curative treatment methods have been tried and have failed in their ultimate goal of saving the person's life. Rather than continuing with curative treatment that is unable to cure, or attempting to prolong a person's life when the physical quality of that life is severely limited, the medical focus will often change to comfort care. Comfort care is when the focus of treatment changes from the disease to the patient. Rather than unsuccessfully treating the disease, the doctor treats the patient to make him as comfortable as possible. The actual disease is virtually ignored, except for any uncomfortable symptoms, such as pain or shortness of breath, which are aggressively treated.

Comfort is generally viewed and addressed in four specific areas: physical, mental, emotional, and spiritual. In hospice care, various professional disciplines generally take the lead in assessing and treating the person in the various comfort areas. Physicians, nurses, and nurse aides all address the physical comfort of the patient. Social workers and bereavement counselors address both the mental and emotional comfort of the patient and family. Chaplains, pastors, priests, and rabbis generally lead in the area of spiritual comfort of both the patient and family. By viewing medical treatment from a comprehensive comfort view, the patient, and not the disease, becomes the focus of everyone's work.

Pain Control

Over my years, I have never met anyone who enjoyed pain. On the contrary, the majority of people I have met have a great fear of pain, and that fear is doubled or tripled for those facing terminal illness. Much of the continued debate regarding physician-assisted suicide is based upon an unrealistic fear of pain associated with the dying process. The reason I call this an unrealistic fear is because there is no reason for anyone to suffer uncontrollable pain in the advancing progression of his or her disease.

In recent years, there have been great leaps in the field of pain control. The medical community has made progress in the types of pain medication available, the variety of medication administration methods, and their understanding of the importance of pain control for their patients. However, if you listen to people, they will tell you about friends or family members who have unfortunately experienced out-of-control pain.

There are a variety of reasons why someone might experience unbearable pain, and following is a partial list of some of the most common ones.

The patient and family are afraid of certain medications.
Many people are as afraid of morphine as they are of the pain itself. I am unable to tell you how many times I have personally heard patients or family members claim a "morphine allergy" when none existed. They will often cite a hospitalization when a narcotic was given for pain and the result was as an undesirable reaction. In the vast majority of these cases it appeared that the amount of pain medication they were given was too much for the specific pain they were experiencing. This resulted in excessive sleepiness, confusion, or hallucinations. These people then believe their problem is with the narcotic, and not necessarily with the amount of the medication they were given.

My experience with end of life care is that an actual allergic reaction to morphine or other narcotics is very rare. When the dosage of pain medication is accurately adjusted by a nurse, following the orders of the physician, to the amount and type of pain experienced by the patient, the side effects are minimal. I remember one patient in particular who was on the highest dosage of morphine I had ever seen, but it matched her pain so well that she was able to do nearly anything she wanted without any adverse effects. Her physician specialist, whose office was nearly 100 miles away, was so amazed with the report that he considered making a house call to see this woman who, while on so much morphine, functioned as well as she did. He himself had never witnessed anyone on that much morphine alive, let alone walk around her house unassisted. (By the way, he never made the house call, but did talk to her on the phone several times).

The patient's physician is unfamiliar with prescribing higher dosages of pain medication.
Simply put, some physicians do not have very much experience with pain control and are frightened to give over a particular dosage. I am not necessarily being critical of the physician, but if she specializes in a particular area, pediatrics for example, she may not have much experience with end-of-life issues. Thankfully, there are more and more physicians offering pain control consultation to other physicians.

I believe it is a very good idea to talk with your physician about his or her philosophy and practice when it comes to end-of-life pain control. If you don't receive an answer that is pretty close to *"I may not be able to keep you completely pain free, but I will do my best to get you as close as I possibly can while balancing your quality of life as you define it,"* I would

29

suggest finding another physician to manage your pain control issues. A good place to start looking is with your local hospice organization. All Medicare certified hospices must have a Medical Director, and usually they are some of the best regarding pain control. He may work directly with you, consult with your physician, or point you towards a physician who is good in the area of pain control.

Some people believe that pain is supposed to be a part of the dying process.
Personally, I am so sensitive to pain that I do not want to experience even the slightest amount of discomfort. However, I have spent time working with many people who had resigned themselves to an expectation that pain will be there no matter what. Some people also see pain as a means of character development during this stage of life. I appreciate how a person can develop these views, but the severity of unchecked pain with certain diseases goes beyond the positive benefits that some people hope to gain.

Lack of information and understanding on pain management can result in inconsistent pain control. Unless a person has been taught about the process of pain management, he will often follow an "as needed" model. What I mean is that unless a person is experiencing pain, he may be reluctant to take his next scheduled dosage until he feels the pain returning. Therefore, he may spend several hours a day trying to play catch-up on pain control.

Pain medication is generally provided in two forms: long-acting and fast-acting. The long-acting is generally designed to provide a base-level of pain control. The medication may be in the form of time-release pills, patches you wear on your skin, or an IV pump. The amount of long-acting medication will be gradually increased as the disease process continues and as the person's body becomes accustomed to that particular amount of medication (tolerance). The type of long-acting medications may be changed as the amount of pain a person is experiencing increases.

Fast-acting medication is designed for controlling pain that "breaks through" the base level. Pain does not remain constant but is more akin to stock market graphs. Pain may drop a little and then spike and then drop down again. Fast-acting pain medication is rapidly absorbed into the bloodstream to control break-through pain in a matter of minutes. It comes in a variety of forms: tiny tablets, liquid drops, injections for IV tubes, and IV pumps. If you are taking fast-acting pain medication, you will want to keep close records of when and how much you are taking. Your nurse will have the physician adjust your long-acting medication when you are taking over a certain amount of fast-acting medication on a regular basis.

The important thing I want to get across in this section is you do not have to experience out-of-control pain. The time to talk to your doctor about the issue of pain control is NOW. Do not wait until you are experiencing pain to talk to him; do so before you are experiencing excessive pain. Learn his philosophy about treating pain, and if necessary find another physician who will treat your pain as aggressively as possible. As I have often said in hospice settings, "We don't aggressively treat the disease, but we do aggressively treat the pain."

Nausea

Nausea is often a companion of the terminally ill. Sometimes it goes along with a particular illness, but often it is a side effect of chemotherapy or narcotic pain medications. Nausea can be particularly frustrating when the person still has their appetite and wants to eat. There are several things one can try doing to reduce the nausea.

The first thing I always recommend is for the person to consult with their physician or nurse. They can help you accurately assess the likely cause of the nausea and whether a medication adjustment can be made to ease the nausea or whether an anti-nausea medication should be started. Most hospice patients I have worked with found satisfactory relief from a medication called Compazine, though I've seen physicians prescribe other medications when Compazine did not seem to do the trick.

You can also try a variety of different dietary and environmental modifications to ease the nausea. For example, many people find they are unable to eat meats, especially red meats, as they once could. In these situations, switching to chicken, turkey, lean pork, or luncheon meats may help keep the nausea at bay. Others find that just the smell of foods, especially when they are being cooked, can trigger a bout of nausea.

I remember one farm family who insisted on eating their traditional Illinois-German meals every day no matter what. Unfortunately, the elderly husband who had terminal cancer was experiencing severe nausea that was triggered by the cooking process. Although he dictated that he wanted roast beef with potatoes, carrots, onions and lots of gravy, he found himself unable to eat a bite or even remain in the house by the time the meal was served due to the overwhelming cooking odors. I was able to help this family find a relatively simple solution by utilizing their summer kitchen.

Most old farmsteads in the area had a summer kitchen, though rarely are any used on a regular basis since the advent of modern stoves and air conditioning. This family still used their summer kitchen for canning vegetables in the summer and fall, and was able to start using it for cooking the big family meals to keep the smells out of the house. The wife would dish up the plates and bring them inside, and her husband was able to eat what he wanted for several more weeks.

He also found another trick that he shared with me on a follow-up visit. He eventually reached the point where the smells from his plate began to cause him problems, so he would simply have his plate placed in the refrigerator for a few minutes prior to eating, and the chilling reduced the odor to a manageable level.

If you do not have a summer kitchen in your backyard, you can still accomplish the same results by improvising with what you have. I have had families grill outside on the propane grill, cook in the garage with a Coleman camping stove, and even use the neighbor's kitchen. I had one family who definitely had the right idea. The wife was the patient, the husband was the caregiver, and the husband hated to cook. They were not satisfied with their local meals-on-wheels, but did enjoy eating at a little restaurant a few blocks from their home. He simply went down to the restaurant, got one of their menus, and placed his order from home. He then drove to the diner, and by the time he walked in the door, the meal was ready. The diner had a wide selection, and the couple sampled everything available and never seemed to get tired of their meals. When his wife became too ill for him to leave her alone, the diner went out of their way to make sure this couple continued to be their best customers ever.

When it comes to food odors, many prepared foods and fruits have little to no smell at all and can be eaten without incident. Breakfast cereals, yogurt, bagels with cream cheese, lunchmeats, canned and fresh fruits can often be added to one's diet as needed to satisfy hunger without triggering a bout of nausea. Most people do best with foods that are cold and sweet. I would encourage you to experiment with different foods, both fresh and processed, and see what works best for you and your family.

Constipation

As with nausea, constipation can be a constant and undesirable companion of the terminally ill, often as a side effect of narcotic pain medication. Constipation can be more than a discomfort; it can become a serious problem. Remember this simple phrase, "What goes in needs to come out." Granted, this phrase is easier said than done, because as a person progresses in their illness their bodily systems can become unpredictable. As their appetite decreases their output also decreases. And, as one nurse told me, when there is less in the pipeline, there is less to move it through.

If you are experiencing constipation be sure and inform your nurse or physician. A simple rule of thumb is to always notify your nurse if you ever go more than three days without a bowel movement. During my time in hospice, every staff member with our agency had two questions they would ask every patient when they saw them: How is your pain, and how are your bowels? We wanted to make sure both were OK all of the time. If your nurse or physician is not asking you these two questions, make sure you give them the answers every time you see them. There are many things that they can offer, from mild to potent, to keep your bowels moving as they need to.

A hospice nurse passed on to me one of my favorite constipation concoctions, and I have passed it on to many others. It is simply known as "The Recipe." Now, don't be thinking about that particular recipe from *The Waltons* television program in the 1970s – That is a different kind of recipe that we will not be getting into in this book. This recipe is simple and effective.

Take one part 100% bran flakes and crush them in a bowl. Add one part applesauce and one part prune juice and mix well. That's it! You can eat it cold or warm, by itself or with a meal. As far as how much to eat, I will leave that up to common sense and your nurse to determine, but it is tasty and it works.

If you are taking any over the counter medication for constipation, please be sure and let your nurse or physician know exactly what you are taking and how often. It is quite important for them to know, especially when they are considering modifications to your treatment plan.

Dehydration

As a person progresses in their illness, their body becomes weaker. It is easy to see these changes externally as a person becomes unable to perform the tasks that only a few weeks earlier they might have easily done. What is harder to see are the changes on the inside. The person's organs, such as heart, stomach, liver, and kidneys, also become weak as the illness progresses; however, because we cannot readily see them we seldom think of them.

One sign of the internal progression of the disease is a decrease in how much the person is drinking. We can see a person reduce their fluid intake from several glasses a day to only a few ounces. It is often at this point when someone in the family over-personalizes this reduction in drinking and sounds the "dehydration alarm." It usually goes something like this, "Oh my, if he doesn't drink more than that he is going to get dehydrated, and we can't let that happen."

Before I go any further, let me ask the question, "What is dehydration?" Dehydration is when body fluids drop below levels needed to maintain a particular state of health. I like describing dehydration by using a lake as an example. Along a river is a lake, and when everything is going well whatever amount of water flows into the lake also flows out. We might even say that such a lake is stable. Now, what would happen if something changed and the amount of water flowing in did not match the amount going out? Problems. The lake would be out of balance. Let's take a look at a couple of quick examples.

Imagine if the same amount of water went into the lake, but more water was going out, as if a dam broke. It wouldn't take long until all the water drained from the lake. This is kind of like the dehydration that occurs when you get the flu and spend all your time in the bathroom. More fluids are leaving your body than is going in. Another dehydration possibility is if the same amount of water is leaving the lake, but not enough is going into it, such as in a drought. This example is similar to someone who is unable to drink enough, such as people trapped in the desert. My final example is when more water is going into the lake than is able to leave. This would result in a flood. This over-hydration can occur in people, as I'll explain in just a moment.

Let's go back to our terminally ill person. As a person approaches the end of life, we often see them drinking only tiny amounts of liquid, and we can easily over-personalize with the situation and say, "If I only drank a few ounces of water a day I would become dehydrated," and that would be true. If you, with normal kidney output, only drank a few ounces a day, then your "lake" would be dry in no time at all. However, the terminally ill person nearing the end of life does not have normal kidney output because of the progression of their disease.

Remember when I spoke about internal organs becoming weaker? As the organs become weaker, they cannot do their jobs as they once could. Consequently, the kidneys process less and less urine, so there is less and less water leaving the body or "lake." A physician once explained to me that when the kidneys slow down they send a message to the brain telling the person not to drink as much, because the kidneys cannot handle the job. The brain generally does this by telling the person that they are not thirsty. Thus, reduced input equals reduced output, and the person's fluid levels are relatively stable.

Now, what would happen if a family member does not understand how this process works and sees their loved one drinking less and less? They will likely panic over fears of dehydration. Moreover, in their panic they might do whatever they can think of to push fluids. They may use guilt to get the terminally ill patient to drink more, or use manipulation to get other family members to push fluids as well. They may even pressure the physician to order IV fluids to "make sure they don't dehydrate." Unfortunately, such practices can be quite detrimental to the patient. Remember in my lake example of more water going into the lake than was going out? It resulted in a flood. That is exactly what happens in the human body when there are too many fluids—we have a flood. I remember one case where a panicking family convinced the doctor to start IV fluids, and as a result the woman swelled with fluids to the point that her skin become overly tight and began tearing. It was very painful for the patient and very difficult to watch.

Whenever I am working with a family, I always try to take as much time as is needed to help everyone understand this process. A well educated family can avoid wasting energy on fears of dehydration, and can properly focus on keeping their loved one comfortable: physically, mentally, emotionally, and spiritually.

Artificial Feeding

Similar to the issue of dehydration, a family can have many questions about the issue of artificial feedings. Before I get started, let's first explore the basics of nutrition for a moment. Why do we eat? The answer is to provide our bodies with the energy necessary to sustain a reasonably healthy life. How much do we need to eat? Good question. There are many factors involved in determining that answer, but an over-simplified answer may be, "as much as we need." During our lifetimes, our bodies require varying amounts of food to keep us healthy. For example, just look at any child going through a growth spurt. They appear to eat all food in sight, but don't become overweight. On the other hand, some of us can just look at a piece of chocolate cake and appear to gain weight. As we approach the end of life due to disease, our physical and nutritional needs change. Typically, our bodies don't require the same amount of energy as earlier, because we spend more time sitting in chairs and lying in beds. We simply are not as active, and thus conserve energy. Also, our metabolism changes, and as it slows down we don't waste energy as when our metabolism was higher.

Another factor that results in a person eating less during this time is the fact that our internal organs are becoming weaker. In the section on dehydration, I spoke about the various internal organs becoming more tired and being unable to work as they once did. Well, the same is true regarding the stomach. A hospice nurse once explained it to me this way. As a person approaches their final weeks, they typically become increasingly tired in all their muscle groups. They cannot walk as they once did, their hands do not have the same grip, and their eye muscles become easily fatigued. If the disease process affects all muscle groups, then why wouldn't the stomach be affected in a similar manner? Isn't it primarily a big bag of muscle designed to churn food for digestion? She explained that the stomach cannot handle meals like it once could, so it sends a message to the person's brain telling it not to send as much food, and the brain generally does this by telling the person they are not hungry. Consequently, the person will continue to reduce the amount of food they are eating, often to the point of not eating at all.

As with the fear of dehydration, some family members can panic with the fear their loved one is starving to death. In response to this fear, they may use guilt to try and get the person to eat, but unfortunately this effort can have several serious drawbacks. To me, the biggest drawback is that the patient may spend his last days or weeks struggling with added guilt over eating something they have no desire to eat nor do they need. Another problem is what does the stomach do with food it cannot digest? It basically has two options: send the food back where it came from through vomiting, or release inadequately digested food into the intestines where, depending upon the unique condition of the patient, can cause a variety of problems.

Sometimes the issue of whether to place a feeding tube is discussed. Let me make myself clear, there is a time and a place for feeding tubes in the aggressive care of people, but in most cases feeding tubes are not of significant benefit to those who are terminally ill. For those who are dying, the body does not need food as it once did. Yes, a person will lose weight, and for the most part, that is all right. It is a part of the dying process. At best, we are often complicating a person's life with either an uncomfortable tube down their throat or a tube surgically implanted into their abdomen to give them a brief extension on their life during the time when they are generally most ready to let go. Again, it has been my experience over the years that when people understand the nutritional process of the terminally ill, have the opportunity to ask questions, and receive reassurance that they are not starving their loved one, then the issue of eating takes its proper place among the priority issues for the patient and family.

Oxygen

Oxygen is commonly used with terminally ill patients as a means of comfort. As a disease continues to progress, it takes a physical toll on the person's body, and one common effect is shortness of breath. Oxygen can help a person feel a bit more energetic, within reason, and feel better rested. Often when a person starts using oxygen, they may only use it for short periods of time, especially if it is hot and humid outside. The person may then increase their use of oxygen by sleeping with it at night to feel better rested when they awake. In some cases, a person may choose to use oxygen continuously in latter stages of their disease.

On occasion, a patient or family member may fear that the patient is becoming addicted to the oxygen. Let me reassure you that your loved one cannot become addicted to oxygen. The air that you and I breath is composed of 21% oxygen, and an oxygen tank or concentrator is only supplementing their normal breathing with a stream of pure oxygen. If a patient is increasing her use of oxygen it is most likely because her lungs are unable to absorb the oxygen as she once could. The concentrated oxygen makes it easier for her to get the amount she needs to feel comfortable.

Sometimes a person may complain of dryness in their nose due to the oxygen. If this happens to you, contact your medical equipment provider and have them attach a water humidifier to the concentrator or tank. You will need to fill the humidifier with distilled water daily, but you should notice relief with the additional moisture. If for some reason this does not seem to help, check with your nurse about rubbing a small amount of a water-based lubricant, such as KY Jelly, in your nostrils to provide moisture. Do not use petroleum jelly with oxygen equipment.

Medical Equipment

There are a variety of items available to help a family safely and comfortably maintain a loved one at home. Virtually any piece of equipment you typically find being used for patient care in a hospital or nursing home setting can be provided in the home through a durable medical equipment provider. The most common equipment found in the home can include quad canes, walkers, wheel chairs, hospital beds, various air mattresses, over bed tables, over bed trapeze, bedside commodes, toilet stool risers, bath tub chairs, oxygen concentrators and/or tanks, and lift chairs. Not every patient has every item, and equipment is typically added one piece at a time, as the patient needs them.

At times a patient may resist certain pieces of equipment such as oxygen or a hospital bed, because they are using the equipment to gauge the progression of their illness. I remember one lady who, even though her traditional bed was very uncomfortable despite having propping pillows all over it, she refused to allow a hospital bed to be brought into her home. When I listened to her reason why she was refusing, she told me that when her husband finally had to be in a hospital bed that his physical condition declined rapidly. She had convinced herself that if she could stay out of a hospital bed she could keep her disease at bay. I helped this lady realize that if she needed to gauge the progression of her illness, that there were much more accurate ways to do so. She eventually agreed to use the hospital bed and found it much more comfortable.

Caring for the Caregiver

One of the most important roles in end of life care is that of the primary care giver. The caregiver, generally the most involved individual in providing care, knows the most about the patient's condition, and is vital to maintaining a person in their home. When I meet with a family, I always try to pay as close attention to the caregiver as I do to the patient. I know that maintaining the caregiver's health is sometimes even more important than that of the patient. If something happens to the caregiver, and another caregiver is not available, then it will be very unlikely that the patient will be able to remain in their home environment. So, as the social worker, I always strive to monitor and support the caregiver the best I am able.

For Caregivers

Let me take a moment and directly talk to the caregiver. First, thank you for the sacrifice you are making in providing care for the patient. I do not know your specific relationship to the patient, whether it is a spouse, parent, child, sibling, or friend, but your role and commitment is very important. I often describe the caregiver as the quarterback of a football team. A quarterback is on the field, calls the plays, and directs a team of players all working towards the same goal. As the primary caregiver, you are the most involved, you make decisions regarding care of the patient, and you coordinate a team of family, friends, and health care professionals in providing for the needs of the patient. That is a big task, to say the least. It will be overwhelming at times. You will become emotionally and physically drained. Moreover, it is vitally important for you to remember you cannot do it all yourself.

One of the most frequent conversations that I have with caregivers is to caution them about trying to do it all. I have worked with hundreds of families, and I believe I speak with credibility when I say even you cannot do it all. If you try to do it all you will exhaust yourself to the point that you may need your own caregiver – I have personally seen this happen. If you are in the early stages of care, you very well may be able to personally meet all of the patient's needs, but as the patient's disease progresses and his needs increase, you will need help.

In talking with caregivers, many times they believe that if they need help in providing care that they must be falling short on their commitment. I remember one wife who told me with tears in her eyes that if she accepted help that she would have failed her husband. She stated with determination that she would do everything by herself if it killed her. Well, in her case, it did not kill her, but she did end up in a hospital and the patient was forced to leave the home due to a lack of a replacement caregiver.

When I talk with caregivers about letting others help them with the various duties, I am often told there is no one who can help them. As you read this section, you may be thinking the same thing. If so, please get a piece of paper and pencil and let me lead you through a brief exercise. **First**, list everyone in your immediate family: adult children, brothers, sisters, parents, in-laws, nieces and nephews. Do not eliminate anyone from this list at this time. Just build the list. **Then,** add to the list all of your neighbors and your friends with whom you keep in regular contact either by telephone or in person. **Next,** add to this list friends that you have from your church or any civic or community organizations. Again, do not eliminate anyone from the list at this time. **Finally,** add to your list relatives and friends whom you see less frequently and who may live some distance away.

Second, we are going to divide your list into two groups. The first group we will call the **"A List"** and it will be made up of people who are available for helping out on a short notice. They will generally be people who live relatively close to you and at some point during the day, evening, or night would be available to help if a need arose. Your **"B List"** will be composed of people who would be more likely to help if they had some advanced notice from a few hours to a few days. Now, go through your list and write either an **"A"** or a **"B"** next to every name.

Third, we are going to divide your list according to various tasks that need to be completed. Again, if you are in the early stages of care, you may not need any assistance at this time, but I am a firm believer in planning for the future, rather than letting future needs sneak up on us resulting in a crisis. Make a list of the types of tasks that need to be completed to keep your household and the patient's needs up to standard. Some common task areas include the following: vacuuming, laundry, cooking, grocery shopping, outdoor maintenance and lawn care, sitting with the patient while you are out, night time assistance, transportation, answering the telephone, and helping out if the patient falls and you cannot get him up off the floor. As the situation progresses, the emotional and physical strain will increase, and a caregiver's ability to keep up with all of these tasks will suffer. However, by delegating some of these tasks, either occasionally or permanently, a caregiver can keep her strength up to a level that allows her to keep performing her priority tasks.

As you look over your list you may see some people who have to work, take care of their own families, or in your opinion are too old to help. Do not discard your family and friends too quickly. If you let someone know that you have a specific need that can be done according to their schedule, it is amazing how often they can find the time to do it. Also, do not discount the elderly in providing assistance. I know of several senior citizens that were tickled to help with tasks around a house. One lady I knew would vacuum the high traffic areas of her neighbor's house every week. She would also dust the living room and dining room, which were the rooms that most visitors would see. Another elderly lady loved doing laundry. She would come over to the patient's home and find the baskets setting by the washer and dryer. She would wash, dry, fold, and iron two to three times a week to keep the loads smaller. Another lady I knew was in her 90s and was a trained hospice volunteer. She could not help with many tasks, but would visit her assigned patients once a week for a 2-3 hour visit. She would sit with the patient while the caregiver got out of the house to either run a few errands or take some time for herself. Sometimes she would even bring over some fresh-baked goodies for everyone to enjoy.

Do not hesitate to ask people to help you with either big or little things. Do not let pride get in the way of receiving needed help. Often, when I talk with various family members following a crisis, they tell me that they would loved to have helped the caregiver but no one asked and they did not want to seem pushy. People enjoy helping others, so let them help. Give them a specific task to perform. As for those family members who live more than an hour away, ask them to come for an all day or weekend visit, and while they are there take some time for yourself. As long as they know whom to call if they need some help, I am sure they will be more than happy to help you in this way.

For Family & Friends of the Caregiver

Let me take a moment to speak to the family members and friends of the caregiver. Do not take the caregiver for granted. This is a very tough job that can overwhelm a person just like a tidal wave. Pitch in and help the caregiver even if you have not been asked to do so. Realize that the caregiver can easily become emotionally upset due to multiple factors including physical demands, emotional exhaustion, sleeplessness, and anticipatory grief to name a few.

One of your important tasks is to keep the caregiver as healthy as possible. Sometimes a caregiver can be attacked by family from out of town who are overwhelmed with their own grief issues (see *"Saviors from Out-of-Town"* under the section on Grief). If the caregiver is being attacked, stand up for her and protect her. Sometimes a caregiver can find herself on the edge of collapse, and when an unwarranted attack comes, you may find yourself with a caregiver who says "I quit."

If you find the caregiver having a difficult time coping with anticipatory grief, contact your nurse or hospice social worker for assistance. They are trained to help caregivers cope with the multiple roles of family member and caregiver. Remember, it is better to address a problem earlier rather than waiting for a crisis to unfold.

Items of Importance

As you find yourself facing terminal illness, there are several important issues that you should consider addressing. Actually, everyone, regardless of their physical condition, should consider each of these below items of importance. The reason I bring these up for discussion is that most people avoid dealing with issues that center around the end of one's life. Maybe most people can avoid these decisions for the time being, but if you are facing terminal illness, then you need to examine each of these items and determine how you want to address them.

Advanced Directives

During the 1970s there were several high profile cases involving individuals who had been in car accidents or had strokes and were kept alive on artificial life support against their families' wishes. Seeing families go through the ongoing anguish of court battles to allow a person to be "unplugged" was too much for many people, including lawmakers. As a result, nearly every state has instituted various forms of advanced directives to allow people to express their desires for health care at the end of their life. Because each state has their own set of laws regarding advanced directives, you need to contact your physician, home care or hospice organization, local hospital, nursing home, senior citizens center, or attorney for specific forms and rules as it applies to your state. As for the below information, I will be talking about the laws in the State of Illinois at the time this book was written as I understand them. Remember, I am not a lawyer, nor do I play one on TV, but I am a social worker and have explained this information to many families. With that in mind, let's look at the various advanced directives.

Do Not Resuscitate (DNR) Order

The DNR or "No Code," as it is sometimes called, is a physician's order stating that if the person's heart stops beating that medical personnel are not to attempt to restart the heart, but they are to allow the person to die at that time. Generally, this is only done when either (1) the physician expects that death is very near and death-delaying procedures are not warranted, or (2) when the patient has a terminal illness and the patient has expressed to the physician that he does not want any heroic measures at the time of his death. A DNR order does not mean that the person is unable to receive any necessary medical care, it simply means that when the person's heart stops, and they are clinically dead, that they will be allowed to die at that time without any heroic measure.

The decision to ask for a DNR order can be distressing for both the patient and family. I would suggest that the patient and family discuss the subject of what to do when the heart stops. I realize that this will not be easy, especially if it has never been discussed before, however it is something that needs to be addressed. Imagine the family trauma that can occur when life-prolonging measures are either performed or not performed to the shock and anger of various family members. Regardless of how tough it can be to discuss, it is something that needs to be decided sooner, not later.

I have found a relatively easy way to introduce the subject to a patient. I simply ask the patient what he would want us to do when it is his time to go and his heart stops. Would he want us to let him go at that time, or does he want us to start CPR, call the ambulance, be rushed to the Emergency Room, and have all measures taken to preserve his life. When introducing this option to patients and their families, I always explain what happens once CPR is started.

I have found that many people believe that if CPR is started that it will be continued for a period of time, and if their heart doesn't start beating on it's own that they will simply stop the CPR. Unfortunately for many people, this is not what happens. If you have ever gone through CPR training, you know that the first thing you do is call 911. CPR is not really designed to get the heart beating again, but it is to keep oxygen circulating in the body to prevent biological death from lack of oxygen. Once the ambulance arrives and takes the patient to the emergency room, the patient will often receive mechanical life support of some sort as determined by the ER physician. This is often the last thing that terminally ill people want to have happened to them, especially if they are already in hospice. When this is explained, nearly all terminally ill people choose to receive a DNR order.

To receive a DNR order you can either contact your physician directly, or you can talk to your nurse and she will usually be able to arrange it for you. A copy of the DNR order will be kept in your chart at the physician's office, and additional copies need to be available to everyone who provides healthcare services to you: hospice or home care organization, medical equipment company, local hospital, and other consulting physicians.

Items of Importance

Living Will

A Living Will is statement of your intentions of what you would like to have happen or not happen in regards to your health care if you were unable to speak for yourself. Living Wills are NOT the same thing as a Last Will and Testament for dividing up your property upon your death. On the contrary, they are only in effect while you are alive and if you are unable to speak for yourself for whatever the reason.

Most living wills are worded to allow a person who is terminally ill to avoid life-prolonging measures. Below is the primary paragraph from a living will form I frequently use with my patients in Illinois. I think you will find the intent fairly easy to understand and meets the needs of most terminally ill individuals.

If at any time I should have an incurable and irreversible injury, disease, or illness judged to be a terminal condition by my attending physician who has personally examined me and has determined that my death is imminent except for death delaying procedures, I direct that such procedures which would only prolong the dying process be withheld or withdrawn, and that I be permitted to die naturally with only the administration of medication, sustenance, or the performance of any medical procedure deemed necessary by my attending physician to provide me with comfort care.

Living Wills can be obtained from hospitals, nursing homes, senior citizen centers, office supply stores, hospice organizations, and attorneys. You do NOT have to go through an attorney to complete one, nor does it need to be notarized, but it will need to be witnessed by someone who is completely independent to your decision. A family member, anyone in your will, or someone routinely providing health care or custodial services to you, should not witness the living will. Have a neighbor, friend, pastor, or someone from your church be your witness.

Once you complete your living will, have several photocopies made and give them to your physician, your hospice or home care organization, medical equipment provider, local hospital, and all members of your immediate family. Again, just like with a DNR order, you want people to understand your wishes long before a crisis situation happens. Also, I believe it is a good idea to have a few extra copies made and kept in a handy place in your home, so if someone else needs a copy of your living will you can give them one immediately.

Power of Attorney for Healthcare

A Power of Attorney for Healthcare (POAH) is a very valuable advanced directive that I believe everyone needs to have, regardless of his or her age or current physical condition. Let me explain my concern by giving you a few examples. Let's say you were in a car accident and are in a coma. Who will make healthcare decisions for you? How about if you are an older adult who has a stroke affecting memory and decision making, and your family strongly disagrees as to the type of care you should receive. Who will make healthcare decisions for you? Finally, what if you went into surgery for a routine operation and the unthinkable happens and you come out of the operating room on life support and in an irreversible coma. Does anyone have the legal authority to disconnect the life support in accordance with your living will? These three examples are real situations that I was involved with in some fashion in recent years. They do happen. Am I trying to scare you? NO, but I am very committed to helping people prepare for end of life issues, because regardless of how we feel about it, you can't escape death and taxes.

Let me ask you some blunt questions to help you prepare for completing a POAH form. When you are unable to make healthcare decisions on your own, who do you specifically want to make decisions for you? Who will make decisions closest to the way you want the decisions made? If there is a family dispute regarding treatment, who do you want to have the final say as to what happens to you? Are you thinking of specific people? The person best for the position of POAH may be a spouse, child, sibling, or even a friend. Make a list of all the people you would consider being your POAH, and then put that list in order from best person on down. When you get to this point you are ready to get the forms and start filling in the blanks.

You can get POAH forms from the same places that you can get Living Will forms. Many times they are bundled together, so if you get one you will likely get the other. Most POAH forms I have seen have the same basic components. First, they want to know who you want to be your POAH. Second, they want to know who else you want to be POAH if your first choice is unable to assume the position. Usually you can list several people on the form, though each person will act alone as POAH. You NEVER want more than one person to be POAH at any given time. If you have more than one person acting as POAH and they disagree, they can easily end up in court fighting over legal guardianship and spending literally thousands of dollars. Third, you will need to initial a statement that is essentially a mini living will. There are other components to a POAH form and they very from state to state, but these three components are the main ones to think about prior to completing the form.

Again, just like on the Living Will, you will need to have non-family witnesses, but you do not have to have it notarized or prepared by an attorney. I don't want to drive this point into the ground too much, but please take my suggestion and complete a POAH. On a personal note, a member of my family did not have a POAH, and she expected her children to get along and make decisions together. Guess what, that didn't happen. It turned into a court battle over guardianship with so many hurt feelings that it caused a permanent split in the family between people who had been very close for years. Could a POAH have kept this family rift from happening? Only God knows the answer to that, but I can't help but wonder how things could have been different if she had completed one.

Power of Attorney for Finance

What the POAH does for healthcare decisions, the Power of Attorney for Finance (POAF) does for financial decisions. If you cannot make healthcare decisions due to an illness or injury, then who is going to make your financial decisions? Who will pay your bills? Who will manage your checking and savings accounts? Who will manage your mutual funds or stocks and bonds? Who will sell property if you need to liquidate for covering various expenses?

These kinds of decisions cannot just be made and carried out by anyone. Many times family members jump in to make decisions and pay bills and will often do so by signing the patient's name to the form or the check. I don't know how many times I have heard people say, "Mom knows that I do this, and she doesn't mind." Probably in most cases no notices that the family member is doing this. However, this is forgery. I once spoke with an attorney whose aunt was in hospice, and he told me how most people don't realize that they are breaking the law by signing a parent's name to a check, etc. He said where people get in a lot of trouble is when they make financial decisions that other family members disagree with. It can be these disgruntled family members that file charges against the person forging the signature, and in some cases, the person can wind up with a large fine and jail time.

This is where a POAF comes into the picture. A POAF is not as simple as the other advance directives, and it does require the assistance of a competent attorney. Whether you have a little money or a lot, I would recommend at least discussing your situation with an attorney. For those of you who do not have that much money, or do not think that it is worth addressing, I would suggest you at least talk to your banker about other options available to you. He may suggest having another family member's name on the various accounts, so they can take care of financial matters for you when you are unable to do so yourself.

When it comes to a Living Will, Power of Attorney for Healthcare, and Power of Attorney for Finances there is one thing you must always remember. You can ONLY legally complete this when the person is legally competent to make decisions. If you wait too long and a person's mental state deteriorates, then your only course may be Guardianship of the Person and Guardianship of Property. Guardianship is determined by a judge, takes quite of bit of time depending upon the size of the family, is expensive, and can be an absolute nightmare if there is family dissention as to who should be the guardian. So, if the patient is still mentally competent, it is in everyone's best interest to pursue the above mentioned advance directives.

Final Arrangements

For many families, the thought of making final arrangements prior to death is disrespectful, but I would like to open the subject for discussion. There are many things we do prior to death that only take place after death. For example, most people have a will and life insurance, which only go into effect after a death. We may also have various pension plans with survivor benefits that also only go into effect upon a death. We may even have our burial plot and tombstone in place, and we might even know which funeral home we want, but still find ourselves shying away from finalizing any decisions about the funeral and surrounding activities. I realize that the topic can be uncomfortable, but I'm of the opinion that we should not leave so many emotionally charged decisions until we are overwhelmed emotionally with the death of a loved one.

There is a wide range of traditions when it comes to death. Some traditions are religious in nature, while others are more a part of family traditions. I am not going to claim to know all the possible traditions available or even attempt to list them in this book, but I will address some of the more common issues that I believe family members ought to discuss and consider deciding upon prior to death.

To Have a Funeral Or Not?

"I don't want to have funeral. I'm not going to be in that body anymore, and I don't want a bunch of people standing around saying 'Doesn't she look natural.' I won't be natural; I'll be dead." I realize that this quote is rather blunt, but it was made by one of my hospice patients about three weeks prior to her death. Her thoughts echo those of others I have had the opportunity to speak to over the years. Her desire was to have her body removed from the home after her death, cremated, and her ashes scattered in her backyard. No visitation. No funeral. No memorial service.

Her plans were very simple, but also very hard to carry out for a family who was grieving the loss of the family matriarch. They needed to openly grieve; they needed to share in their loss; and they needed to come to the full realization that she was gone. In the case of this family and other ones who did not have any visitation, funeral, or memorial service, the various family members generally have a difficult time dealing with their grief.

One family was left with a need to grieve together, but they were distressed with the dilemma of grandma's final wish not to have any kind of service. Instead of the traditional visitation or funeral, they had what they called an "onion party." One family member hosted the event, and all those attending had to bring a knife, cutting board, and a bag of onions. At the onion party they would tell stories about the deceased loved one and cut onions. If anyone was caught crying they could innocently blame the tears on the onions. I give this family an A+ for creativity in meeting their needs in a difficult situation.

There seems to be a need for these kinds of rituals, and if your desire is not to have one, please discuss the issue with your family. By allowing them the opportunity to grieve, you may be giving them one of the best gifts you can give after you are gone.

Burial or Cremation

What will happen to your body following your death? Is it your tradition to have burial the day of the death? Will you be embalmed for burial? If buried, where will you be buried? Will you be cremated? If cremated, will you scatter your ashes, have them kept in a family member's home, interred in a mausoleum, or buried.

It has been my experience that people have either no opinion or a very strong opinion as to what happens with their body or a loved one's body after death. Because of the emotional involvement, the time to discuss this issue is now, and not later. I have seen bitter family arguments at the time of death as to what is to be done with the remains, and the last thing anyone wants to have happen is a family fight or split over this issue.

If your family has a typical way of handling the remains, and if you intend to follow in the family tradition, then please make your desires known to all key family members. It will give them reassurance in following through with the preparations.

If you intend to break with tradition in some fashion, then it is even more important to share your wishes with all key family members well ahead of time. If someone has been anticipating a particular set of rituals for their grief, any change can be interpreted as a kind of threat that easily results in defensive and accusatory behaviors. Talk to the family members, especially those whom you anticipate might have difficulties with any break with tradition. Share with them your logic in making the choice, and be patient with their response. While any decision is ultimately yours, your patience and persistence in addressing the issue with them will help them in the end.

Funeral Arrangements

Did you know that you can make many of your funeral arrangements from your home? Often funeral directors are able to come to your home with their display books and help you make your funeral arrangements. In addition, if you contact your pastor or priest and ask, they will often come to your home to review your wishes regarding the funeral service. You can review the hymns to be sung, the scripture texts to be read, and any special requests you would like to have included in your funeral service.

Cremation: What to do with the remains?

Cremation offers a variety of options for disposal of the remains that simply are not available with burial. One lady I know intends to have her ashes scattered over her parents' graves and have a small maker placed in between their tombstones. A fellow I knew many years ago, who very much enjoyed his beer, wanted his ashes scattered over Anheiser Bush in St. Louis. While his family was not willing to follow through with his specific request, they did do something very interesting. They had his ashes divided and placed into small vials and distributed to family members who did with the ashes as they wanted. Some kept the vials as a remembrance while others scattered them in a personally meaningful way.

One family had a walnut end table made that was about a two-foot cube. It had places for photographs of the deceased on the outside and a door that opened to reveal the urn of ashes on the inside. Since this memorial table was for a young father who died leaving several school-age children, it offered a specific way for the children to express their loss and grieve for their father at the important mile-markers in their lives. Rather than being a dreaded place of tears, it was a safe-haven for expressing the need for their dad.

Clothing, Jewelry, Personal Effects

If you are going to be buried and have an open casket visitation, are there any particular clothes you want to wear or items you want to have present. For example, is there a particular suit or dress you want to wear, and what is your second or third choice? The reason I ask this is from personal experience with my grandmother's final arrangements. She had picked out her burial dress long before her death, and when the family went to the funeral home they discovered that the colors of the available casket linings did not match the color of the dress. We had no idea what to do next. Luckily, the funeral home director had dealt with this issue many times before and had a supply of beautiful dresses that matched the linings very nicely.

What about jewelry, glasses, a favorite bible, or a special photo that would be displayed in the casket? I remember my grandfather wore his glasses in the casket, because it just wasn't grandpa without his glasses. Just about anything can be displayed inside the casket, but think very seriously about leaving anything of sentimental value in the casket for burial. Once the casket is sealed and buried, everything is in there to stay regardless of how heartbroken someone is regarding a broach, wedding ring, or pair of glasses that meant so much to them. Any item on display in the casket can be removed by the funeral director prior to sealing the casket, and it is perfectly alright to keep family heirlooms in the family and not in the grave.

Distribution of Property

What will happen to your property at the time of your death? I find it an interesting piece of human nature that family members rarely fight over the disbursement of cash, but they will fight worse than cats and dogs over small items loaded with sentimental value. I have seen this happen in my family, and I have watched this happen in other families. What is even more interesting is how often these emotionally valuable items are packed away a few months after the "bloody battle" to acquire them.

Why is it that we do this to ourselves? My hunch is that we are not ready to give up this relationship, and we desperately cling onto tangible items that trigger a desirable memory of the lost relationship. It can be a watch, a vase, a lock of hair, a bottle of perfume, a powder puff, an old candy dish, or even a worn out old chair. If we attach a memory to an item, it can take on a very valuable role in remembering an aspect of the relationship. For example, I have my grandmother's old Huffy lawnmower. At the time of writing these words it is nearly 35 years old. It is well rusted and has had to have some major work done to it, but despite the mechanical frustrations I have an enjoyable time using it to mow my yard. When I was a teenager I used it to mow my grandma's yard. She would stand outside and watch me to make sure I did a good job. I enjoyed those times, and when I mowed the yard yesterday, I was able to go back in time and remember her standing there by her rose bushes with her little dog, Tony. After mowing we would go inside and split a bottle of root beer and talk about all kinds of things. I miss my grandma, and it's amazing how even writing about that little old lawnmower brings a smile to my face and a smile to my heart.

What happen when two people share equal feelings towards such an item? Sometimes they find a peaceful resolution, but sometimes in their grief, they can become quite bitter. This is where the still-living owner of the property can make a positive difference for their family members. One person I know has chosen to begin distributing sentimental items long before her anticipated death. She began by asking her children if there were any items they particularly wanted, and if there was a conflict asked for alternate choices. So far, this system has worked rather well with no serious disputes. Another individual listed all the collectable items in her house and had the children and grandchildren identify items they wanted. If there was a conflict she had the parties work out their own compromise bartering with other items they wanted to have. She copied the final list and distributed it to everyone to make sure everything was correct. When no one voiced any complaints, she had all of them sign the list stating that they agreed to the disbursement, and that they would not challenge it after her death without giving up their share.

When my paternal grandmother died, my dad and aunt gathered all the undistributed items and made relatively equal piles. They then drew names out of a hat to determine who received each pile. As far as I knew, it worked out very well.

Items of Importance

To sum up this section, please do not take for granted that your family will happily divide your earthly possessions. If you are able, make your intentions known and clearly state that you expect respect for your decision. It is amazing how many problems can be avoided by anticipating and addressing them in advance.

Children and Funerals

The question of whether children should attend visitations or funeral services is one that makes many people very uncomfortable. It is natural to want to protect children from anything adults see as upsetting, but when is it appropriate for children to attend funeral events? There is not a simple formula to use to find the answer. There is not a magical age like the height charts at amusement parks.

There appears to be two main factors that must be considered when families make these decisions. The first is the family's relationship with death. Some families are very open in talking about death and view it as a natural and common part of life, just like the birth of a baby. Other families consider any conversation about death or references to it as taboo and to be avoided. If a family is open about death, it may be a very natural step to take children to a visitation. I would recommend limiting funeral services to those children who are mature enough to sit still in a respectful manner. If the family is closed to death, then the uncomfortable conversations and behaviors of the adults at a visitation or funeral may increase anxiety and fear in children who are present.

The second main factor to consider is the child's relationship to death. Is this the first time the child has been exposed to issues of life and death? What is the child's relationship to the deceased? Did the child anticipate the person's death or was the information kept from the child? Is there someone who would be able to give all their attention to the child at the visitation or the funeral?

If the child has been trained as to what death is, how it happens, and what happens to the person after they die, then the child will likely do relatively well at a funeral event. However, if the child has had no training regarding death, then you can have a very anxious child who is unable to cope with the situations and cultural expectations. When the deceased is a close friend or family member, the parents may be unable to focus on the child's needs, and in those cases the child may benefit from a funeral escort. A funeral escort is a family member or friend who is not overwhelmed with their own grief, and is able to focus all their attention on the child. They can answer questions, explain the various rituals, and remove the child from the situation if it becomes overwhelming.

A good approach to take with children and funeral events is to ask the child if they would like to go to the visitation or funeral, and then follow up that question with either "why" or "why not." You can learn quite a bit about a child's readiness for attending such events by their answer to "why." If the child wants to attend, you may want to plan alternatives if the event becomes overwhelming. Again, if you are not able to offer all your attention to the child, then plan for a funeral escort.

Items of Importance

Earlier, I mentioned training children in issues related to death. I have had different people ask me what I mean by training, so I will try to explain it here. Personally, I see death as a part of living. We are conceived, born, grow, age, and die. In addition, as a Lutheran Christian, I believe that death is a transition that we all must go through to spend eternity with God in heaven. At the time of writing this section, my children are 4 and 2 years of age, and we talk about life, death, and faith routinely. When my wife, Shannon, was pregnant with our daughter, we did not keep our son in the dark regarding her pregnancy. We told him that there was a baby in her tummy, and that at one time he was in her tummy, too. As he grew older, we showed him a book with photos of what babies look like inside the womb. We did not make up stories to avoid teaching him the truth about life, and we did not go into specifics of how babies are made – that is for a later talk.

Regarding the other end of the life spectrum, we also openly talk about death. With a surname like Quicksall, we are fascinated with genealogy and family research, and I teach my children about their ancestors, when they lived, and where they are buried. Each Memorial Day we visit the graves of my grandparents and great grandparents and talk about their bodies being in the grave, but their souls are with God in heaven. When we see a dead animal, we talk about the death of the animal's body. We also talk about family members that we long to see again in heaven. My children do not spend all their time talking about death, just like they do not spend all their time talking about babies. We had the opportunity to go to a funeral several months ago, and we looked forward to using this as another step in their training process. When we arrived at the funeral home, my son was disappointed in that there was not a body for viewing, because the deceased was cremated. This surprise led to an unanticipated discussion about different ways bodies that are prepared after death. The other week we went to the Field Museum in Chicago for a mini-vacation. While there, we saw an unwrapped mummy of a child about my son's age. He became quiet and pondered what he saw. I answered immediate questions he had as to why the boy looked the way he did, and then we found a quiet spot to talk more about this unanticipated experience. When we keep the topic of death open for discussion and use opportunities to gradually expose our children to the reality of life and death, they will be much better able to cope with deaths of close family members and friends.

Preserving Your Memories

A few years ago, Michael Keaton played the role of a terminally ill father-to-be in the movie "My Life." In the film, Michael creates a videotape of his life for the child he will never see. Following the release of this movie, many people began recording who they were for future generations. Maybe you don't see yourself making a video, but recording your memories can be priceless gift you give your family.

My father and I are into family history and genealogy, and while my father is still relatively young (75 years old) and seemingly healthy as a horse, he wanted to make sure he recorded important tidbits from his life for his grandchildren who are four and two years old. My dad's project turned into a thirty-some page typed book that I intend to typeset and bind for the grandkids, nieces and nephews.

Items of Importance

Others have done similar projects, either on their own or with the assistance of workbooks available in many bookstores. Some ideas I have seen or heard about include:

- Tape record funny stories or favorite jokes

- Have a family member interview you about your early years, school, military, or work experience

- Go through the old photo album with a tape recorder, and while numbering and describing the photographs, tell the story behind each one

- If possible, go visiting your old home place, school, or work place and describe the memories you have while someone videotapes you on location

- Sit down with relatives from your generation and swap stories while being audio or video recorded

You can easily have a transcript made from your recording by either a professional firm or a starving college student. In 2001, the going rate for transcription was about $2.00 a page, so you should be able to find something comparable.

What you will leave behind is a record of yourself that others will grow to appreciate over the years. As I mentioned earlier, my father and I are into family history and genealogy. Thankfully, my dad's mom made a detailed account of the family history that she knew, but we both kick ourselves for not doing more with other family members who have long since passed away. We have vowed to learn from those missed moments, and I hope you take advantage of the opportunity that you still have to leave a recorded or written legacy.

Alternatives and Herbal Treatments

The popularity of alternative treatments and herbal remedies has been on the rise for several years, and it has had a strong presence among those experiencing terminal illness. I am not going to debate the benefits or problems associated with these various treatments, since many times there are very strong personal emotions attached to taking them. I will simply make two very strong recommendations to you and your family.

Those seeking to make a fast dollar are quick to prey upon desperate people. Please check out the validity of anyone offering a cure to a terminal illness. Ask specific questions and demand solid, empirical research to back up their findings.

Keep your doctor informed about everything thing you put into your body, no matter how natural or common you believe it to be. Many medications originally came from herbs, and herbs can react in a negative way with medications you may be taking. As an example, I was having dinner with an oncologist who shared with me something I would never have thought of. He asked me what vitamin I would likely take if I were sick. I told him my first choice would probably be Vitamin C. He then asked, if I was really sick would I consider taking a higher dose to try and boost my immune system, and I answered that I probably would since I had heard of people taking "mega-doses" when very sick. He then told me that with certain types of cancer, large dosages of Vitamin C could actually make the cancer cells immune to chemotherapy. In other words, a person taking Vitamin C to try and help their body beat the cancer could actually be taking something that will kill them. So, please consult with your physician about any and all alternative and herbal treatments you are taking or are considering taking.

The Three Phases
of Terminal Illness

There are a variety of different ways to describe what people experience as they draw closer to death. There are physical, emotional, mental, and spiritual changes. Sometimes we try to see these changes on a timetable to give us an idea of how much time we have until death occurs. This can be a difficult task and next to impossible to accurately predict.

In drawing from my experiences in hospice, I tend to view the terminally ill patient progressing through three phases that include the introductory phase, work phase, and end phase. There appear to be common activities that take place in these unique phases, which does allow a certain amount of predictability. Because there are so many unpredictable factors that are unique to specific diseases, I do not try to impose a physical time frame on these phases. Instead, I view these phases as landmarks that simply let us know that a person is getting closer to the time of death.

Phase 1 – Introductory Phase

This phase typically begins with the diagnosis of a terminal illness and a physician offering a limited amount of time until the person dies. Ideally, the patient and family should learn this information from the physician, but sometimes they might learn it from someone else, such as a nurse, social worker, chaplain, or family member.

The diagnosis of terminal illness generally comes with a recommendation of palliative care. Palliative care is a term that simply means comfort-only care. In a way, we stop treating the disease and begin treating you, the patient. For example, in cancer treatment, the doctor may have you undergo radiation or chemotherapy that can make you quite sick. There is little regard as to how you feel physically, because the doctor is trying his best to kill the cancer and save your life. However, when you switch from curative treatment to palliative care, then the doctor is not trying to kill the cancer or save your life, but he is trying to make you as comfortable as he can for the time you have remaining. In essence, in hospice we would pay very little attention to the cancer at all. We would generally allow nature to take its course as to the progression of the disease. What we would pay attention to is you: how well you are feeling, whether you are experiencing any pain or discomfort, and whether there is anything we can do to make you more comfortable physically, mentally, emotionally, or spiritually? The focus really does change from a tumor inside your body to you as a person and your family as your primary support system.

During this introductory phase, you may experience a variety of different thoughts and feelings. You may feel absolute shock at the news. You may experience disbelief where you simply cannot believe the information you have just received. You may also feel anger that often stems from fear, anxiety and panic. You may find yourself bargaining for other medical opinions and experimental or alternative treatments as you face the question, do I fight or die?

Often our emotional response during this introductory phase primarily hinges upon our existing relationship with death. Imagine if you will that death is a person who came knocking at your door. As you open the door, he introduces himself and states that he is not coming to take you right now, but that he is simply going to sit in the corner chair and wait for the appropriate time. He tells you to go about your everyday business and not to worry about him. I realize this example may initially seem odd, but please bear with me. With death sitting in the corner of your room, how you react will have a lot to do with your general acceptance of death as a part of life. Some people will calmly accept death at this time in their life, because they have been expecting him. Others may become angry that he came when he did, or may become anxious wondering what kind of an impact his presence will have on their life.

A person's physical condition can vary greatly depending upon the disease. Their condition may be stable with no observable change, and in some cases, they may seem to improve with discontinuing certain treatments and actively treating the uncontrolled pain. I remember one gentleman who continued with his job as a school bus driver although he only had approximately three months to live. I also remember a lady who was able to return to her active lifestyle in the community once the nurses were able to get her pain under control. In most cases, the person does not have a major deterioration in their health during the introductory phase.

Phase 2 – Work Phase

During the work phase, the patient is often experiencing a lot of mental change. The patient has much to absorb

74

regarding his illness, and may decide to take an active role in planning his care and in making future preparations regarding the time of his death. I remember one gentleman in particular who was concerned for his wife. She had relied upon him greatly throughout their marriage, and he wanted to make sure she would be taken care of following his death. He arranged to have all household bills managed by his banker, any future legal matters to be handled by his attorney, and any house maintenance to be performed by a local handyman. He helped her connect with the local senior center and develop relationships with other seniors in her neighborhood. He also arranged for taxi service for her with the bill being sent to the bank. Finally, he made all of his own funeral arrangements with burial to be at a cemetery only a few blocks from their home, so she could easily visit the grave when she wanted. Not everyone carries out his plans as this man did, but it is a great example of what can be done regarding preparations for the future.

Other times, the work that we do during this phase centers on relationships, typically strengthening them or restoring them. I remember one gentleman who had close ties with all of his children. During this phase, he met with them individually reminiscing the fun times they had in the past and he offered them specific words of encouragement to lead them in the future. Another patient I remember fondly was a quite elderly lady who had not been the best mother to her children and some had not spoken to her for years. She either spoke by telephone or wrote in letters to each of them confessing her wrongdoing in their lives and asked for forgiveness and reconciliation before her death. This work was not easy for either her or her children, but the rewards were great, as she was able to restore these broken bonds in the family.

The person will also likely spend time working in the spiritual area. Some people are quite private about their spiritual work while others are more open and sharing. Common spiritual questions that the patient wrestles with include whether their life was worth living, what if anything comes after death, and will they be ready to meet their maker. If have found that those who have a strong and active faith throughout their life often quickly find a sense of peace in the spiritual area. The religious practices that helped them develop a close relationship with God over their lifetime are now used to help them prepare to let go of this world and move into the next. However, those who have avoided spiritual issues throughout their life often struggle with much distress as they come to terms with these big questions. Many times a person has had at least some exposure with a particular church body, and they may want to meet with a pastor or priest to help them with these issues. Other times, a trusted neighbor who is comfortable with both end-of-life and faith-based issues can provide needed comfort and direction. Hospice organizations also have chaplains on their staff who represent the different faiths in their geographical area. The goal of spiritual work is to find a greater sense of peace regarding their relationship with God and knowing that he will accept them with all their imperfections when the time of death comes.

As people work during this phase, they may appear to be withdrawing from family and friends. Sometimes family members become concerned because the patient is not talking with others as they once did or that they appear to be sleeping more. What is likely happening is that the patient is thinking through many of these issues mentioned in the above paragraphs. I often refer to this withdrawal as "head-time."

During head-time, the person is thinking through the issues to find both resolution to problems and a new perspective now that they have a limited life expectancy. A person going through head-time may appear grumpy if you disturb them. They are performing the serious work of thinking through serious issues, so your patience is needed. Often this thinking is done with their eyes closed, so what may appear to be sleep is actually deep thought. Sometimes patients who are in the work phase become exhausted easily, which can be a combination of the emotional energy spent and the physical progression of their disease.

Phase 3 – End Phase

The end phase is when most of the work to be completed has been finished, and the patient's focus turns within. This inward focus seems to have three primary tasks which are to cope with increased symptoms of the disease, rest in the level of peace they have reached, and withdraw from the people and things of this world in preparation for going into the next one.

Sometimes the work of phase two is completed prior to an increase in the symptoms of the disease, while other times the work phase is cut short do to the increase of symptoms. While the symptoms a person experiences are unique to their disease, there are many signs commonly seen as a person draws closer to death. I will discuss this in detail in the next section.

Resting is an important part of the end phase. The person often has very limited energy and is unable to do very much end-of-life work at this time, so they often rest in the peace they have achieved. Sometimes family members are able to do additional work to help the patient experience greater peace. For example, if an estranged family member can be reached and brought to the patient for a time of reconciliation, this may give the patient a greater sense of peace than would have been attainable on his or her own.

The patient is also beginning to detach more from this world and embracing the world to come. Just like a high school graduate begins to shift from his hometown buddies to his college hopes and dreams, so the patient often begins letting go of family and friends and spends a greater amount of time thinking about what is to come. A person who may not have had much spiritual or religious interest during life may take up an interest in preparation for the world to come. I remember one gentleman who at times mocked his wife's religious practices. During my last several visits, I found this man reading his wife's Bible and asking questions about faith. I have to admit I was pleasantly surprised.

Early Signs of Approaching Death

Often the first signs include lack of appetite, lack of energy, general fatigue, and increased sleep. These can be disturbing to family members because often the patient is functioning well in other areas, and we either believe that something else is wrong with them, or we see these as the first signs toward death and we are not ready for that yet. However, these signs are typical and natural as the disease process continues.

Probably the lack of appetite is the single most disturbing sign for both patients and family members. Often the pleasant taste of food changes and nothing seems to be enjoyable. The patient's appetite may fluctuate without predictability and a hungry patient may lose his appetite by the time dinner is prepared. Generally, red meats are the first ones to lose their appeal, followed by other meats, vegetables, and then fruits. Foods with stronger smells go first among patients with nausea. Eventually, solid foods give way to liquids and eventually liquids may stop all together as the kidneys begin to shutdown.

As the patient's disease progresses he will likely experience increased fatigue and an increased need for sleep. The disease is taking a toll on the physical body, and the body is fighting back with all available resources, resulting in physical exhaustion. Naps become a regular habit and may take place after any physical exertion. Some people benefit from the occasional use of oxygen, either by tank or concentrator. Using oxygen after physical activity and during sleep can reduce fatigue for a time by making more oxygen available to muscles and internal organs. Also, increased oxygen to the brain can improve mental functioning and alertness.

Later Signs of Approaching Death

As the disease progresses, it has more of an impact on the body and regulatory functions between bodily systems. Effects of the disease on the heart can result in decreased blood pressure that can in turn cause blackouts if a patient gets up too quickly from a sitting position. Effects on the inner ear can affect the patient's sense of balance resulting in falls. The patient's body temperature can become unstable with fluctuations of two to four degrees either way. Often the family fears that the person may be getting an infection with fever, when in many cases it is simply the failure of the patient's internal thermostat.

There can be many changes in the skin at this time. Color may be one of the most recognizable changes. If the disease begins affecting the liver the person can develop jaundice, with the skin taking an orange cast. In some cases, the orange salts that leach through the skin can rub off on another person or on a washcloth. I was unaware when I first saw this and almost panicked, so I always try to warn family member that this can happen with jaundice and it is nothing to be alarmed about. The skin may also take on a purplish color in the feet and legs when the circulation of blood begins to slow down. Nail beds and hands can also become pale in color with lack of proper circulation. A person's skin may also become thin and begin to breakdown. The person may bruise easily and the skin may tear if handled roughly or if adhesive tape is used repeatedly in a particular area.

The disease process also affects breathing, and the number of breaths per minute can increase or decrease. When breathing increases, it may get as high as 50 breaths per minute, which is caused by upper chest panting. Sometimes this kind of panting is associated with pain, so you need to assess whether the person's pain is under control. Other times breathing decreases and long pauses between breaths can occur. These pauses are called apnea, and can last anywhere from 15 to 90 seconds. Apnea generally occurs during sleep and can be caused by changes in the diaphragm or by congestion in the respiratory tract.

Mental changes can occur during this time, resulting in difficulties with concentration and memory. They may become confused between the present and the past, referring to things from long ago as if they are happening now. Other times they may describe seeing things and people that no one else can see. Common descriptions include family members who have already died, angels, sensations of flying, and a golden city. There are two primary explanations as to these experiences. One explanation suggests that these visions are simply things the patient desires to see and the mind creates images to meet their desires. The other is that the person is having a "crossover" experience where they literally have one foot in this world and one foot in the next, and they are trying to describe and react to what they are experiencing on the other side. If I may express my bias, many of my colleagues and I lean to the crossover explanation based upon our conversations with our patients and family members, but I will leave your decision up to you. But, if your family member begins describing things you do not see or hear, do not panic, as it is a relatively common experience.

Active Dying

Active dying is a term used to describe the final stage when the body systems are actively shutting down. As the heart begins to shutdown, there is often a significant drop in blood pressure, at times not even registering on the blood pressure cuff. Their heart rate can become very rapid, over 150 beats per minute, as the heart stops pumping and is virtually just quivering. Other times, heart rates can become very slow, less than 20 beats per minute.

The patient's body temperature can fluctuate greatly, become very cold or running a fever over 104° F. Also, the patient will often stop drinking liquids, including water, but you can keep their mouth moist and comfortable with a foam swab or damp washcloth. You may also see restlessness in their legs due to lack of oxygen caused by the shutting down of circulation. Breathing also becomes irregular with either long periods of apnea or shallow, rapid breathing that may be reminiscent of a fish out of water.

The person may lose consciousness and be in a semi-comatose state. Their eyes may be open or closed. They may or may not be able to move their body during this state, but often they are aware of what is being said around them. Remember that it does not take any physical effort to lay and listen. Be careful what you say around the patient if they are in a semi-comatose state, but be sure to tell them you love them, that it is ok for them to go, and that you will be all right. They may be able to hear your words of love and encouragement and feel a greater sense of peace about leaving you behind.

Finally, whether they are awake and alert or asleep, your loved one will exhale their last breath, their heart will stop beating, and their body will relax in death. Their eyes may be open or closed, and either way is natural and normal. At this moment I always encourage the families I work with to turn their focus from the empty body and look to the ceiling, put a smile on your face, and wave good-bye to your loved one as they leave this world. Many people who have had near death experiences describe floating at the ceiling looking down on their body and the people in the room. So, if your loved one is at the ceiling getting ready to leave, you ought to give them a final wave good-bye until that day when they welcome you to the other side.

Closing Thoughts

In concluding this book, I want to encourage you with the words of one of my hospice patients: Live until you die. This has been the resounding theme of many of the patients I have worked with over the years. They did not take their diagnosis as the end, but continued to live their lives to the fullest. Rather than dwelling on what they had lost, they focused on what they still had. Live until you die is an attitude and approach to living that is not reserved just to the terminally ill, but is one that all of us can embrace regardless of our circumstances.

I remember a conversation I had with a gentleman who reminded me even though he had only a matter of a few weeks to live that I could die in a car accident that day. He saw himself at an advantage to putting his life priorities in their proper order, while others often wasted the time they have. He encouraged others to live each day as if it could be their last, thus taking advantage of the wonderful opportunities that God offers us each and every day. I encourage each of you to do the same.

About the Author

Larry E. Quicksall is a Marriage & Family Therapist and founder of Christian Counseling Associates of Effingham. He received his Bachelors of Arts degree in Psychology from Eastern Illinois University and his Master of Social Work degree from the University of Illinois. He received his Clinical Social Worker license in 1993.

Larry has worked extensively in several fields of practice including substance abuse prevention, crisis intervention, severe mental illness, terminal illness and hospice care, parental coaching, and marital and family growth and restoration. He is also a member of the adjunct faculty of Lake Land College where he has taught in the field of psychology since 1991. Larry is a professional speaker and trainer in the human services field, and you can view his counseling & speaking website at www.FamilyGrowth.org.

Comments & Suggestions

I hope you found *We Need to Talk* helpful to your situation. If you have any comments, suggestions or stories, please write them in the space below or on a separate sheet and mail it to the address provided. I am very interested in hearing from you.

Sincerely,
Larry E. Quicksall

_____

_____

_____

_____

_____

_____

Your Name:_____

Address: _____

City: _____ State: _____ ZIP: _____

Phone: _____ Email: _____

Mail to: Larry Quicksall
            FamilyGrowth Publishing
            1310 N. Keller Drive, Suite 9
            Effingham, IL 62401